REAL WORLD ECONOMICS

How Deflation Works

Corona Brezina

+6.73
+1.33
+21.64
+14.83
+919
+3.24
+32.47
+11.02
+2.35
+41
+2.06
+021
+2.42
+5.53

ROSEN PUBLISHING

New York

Published in 2011 by The Rosen Publishing Group, Inc.
29 East 21st Street, New York, NY 10010

First Edition

Library of Congress Cataloging-in-Publication Data

Brezina, Corona.
How deflation works / Corona Brezina.
    p. cm.—(Real world economics)
Includes bibliographical references and index.
ISBN 978-1-4358-9465-5 (library binding)
1. Deflation (Finance)—Juvenile literature. I. Title.
HG229.B764 2011
332.4'1—dc22

                                                                2009045292

Manufactured in the United States of America

CPSIA Compliance Information: Batch #S10YA: For further information, contact Rosen Publishing, New York, New York, at
1-800-237-9932.

On the cover: During early 2008, a period of economic recession, many
retailers experienced slow sales. Shoppers cut back on spending due to
uncertain economic conditions.

Contents

INTRODUCTION

Imagine living through an era when prices, instead of rising or staying the same, steadily declined. Suppose an MP3 album download that cost $10 last year drops to $9.60. The next year it falls even further, to $8.65. The year after that, it drops to $7.75, and a year later, the price is just $7.50. In total, that is a 25 percent price decline over four years.

The effect of steadily declining price levels is called deflation. It might not sound like a great deal, but deflation is generally accompanied by a number of negative economic trends. Lower prices lead to lower profits for businesses. Businesses lay off workers and reduce wages. Unemployment levels rise. Even though prices are low, people try not to spend much money. They might not be able to afford new items because their paychecks are also getting smaller, they have lost their jobs, or they are afraid of soon becoming unemployed.

4

They might be worried about the economic situation, so they decide to save money instead of buying.

Deflation generally occurs during an economic downturn. The downturn often begins with the popping of an asset bubble. For example, the stock market might crash or the value of real estate could collapse. This leads to a recession. In some cases, the economic slowdown may cause price drops in some categories of products. When price drops are sustained, and when they occur across a broad range of goods and services, deflation may result.

During a recession, the government takes action to revive the economy. If deflation were an element of the recession, the government would include specific measures to counter deflation. Lowering interest rates, for example, can discourage deflation. More generally, government spending can stimulate the overall economy. Actions that boost the economy also have the effect of reducing deflation.

During a period of deflation, many businesses have difficulty making a profit. Stores often try to lure customers with sharply reduced prices.

Deflation is a very serious economic concern. The Federal Reserve—the central bank of the United States—implements policies intended to prevent any chance of deflation. These policies have been mostly successful. The United States has not experienced a period of prolonged deflation since the Great Depression. If deflation became a threat, the Federal Reserve would set a course to stabilize prices.

CHAPTER ONE
Understanding Deflation

Chances are, you have never personally experienced deflation in the economy. Since the beginning of the twentieth century, average prices have tended to rise. The term for this is "inflation." When deflation occurs, price levels fall. Periods of deflation are much rarer than periods of inflation. The United States last experienced sustained deflation during the Great Depression. Since then, other countries in the world have gone through periods of deflation. Still, deflation is not a common economic trend.

So if deflation happens so rarely, why should we bother learning or worrying about it? The answer is that it is important to recognize possible warning signs of deflation. Though rare, deflation can be extremely harmful to the economy and to people's lives. So it must be guarded against at all costs. Modern countries avoid deflation because economists watch for indications that deflation could occur in the economy. If it appears that there is a danger of deflation, the government takes steps to prevent it.

What Is Deflation?

Deflation is the process by which overall price levels fall. During periods of deflation, average prices of goods and services steadily

Though gas prices generally rise from year to year, they can fall during recessions when consumers cut back on spending, reduce their driving, and demand goes down.

decrease. If you go to the mall, you may notice that prices are slightly lower than they were last month. Deflation is different from price swings, however. It's normal for prices of items to vary and fluctuate. Costs of energy, food, technology, and other goods often go up or down from one month to the next. Deflation is different. Deflation is marked by a long-term trend of falling prices for goods and services. If prices of a broad range of goods and services fall from one year to the next, economists may view this as a warning sign of deflation.

During a period of deflation, the real value of money increases. This may sound impossible. After all, isn't a dollar always worth the same amount? But during deflation, you can buy more with the same amount of money. Say that you spend a certain amount of money on some groceries, a doctor's appointment, and gasoline for your car. Six months later, you'll have money left over after buying those same goods and services. Your money goes slightly further when the economy is experiencing deflation. This means that money is more

9

valuable. To use economic terms, the purchasing power of your money is increased.

More value for your money sounds great. But deflation can be very bad for the overall economy. Most economists view deflation as a negative phenomenon. Lower prices mean lower profits for businesses. In order to generate more sales in a tight economy, manufacturers and retailers may cut prices. This might attract customers, but businesses do not make as much money from selling products at a discount. And even when offering lower prices, businesses still might not make enough money. If this occurs, they may cut production. This means that they make less of whatever product it is that they sell. This can affect businesses of all sizes. Huge corporations might cut production of manufactured goods, such as refrigerators. Small businesses—whether they're flower shops, clothing shops, or dentist offices—may see fewer customers. They may be forced to find ways to reduce the costs of running the business, such as layoffs or lower-quality merchandise or services.

In turn, a slump in business impacts workers. If a business is not growing, it will not hire new workers. People do not receive pay raises. They may even take pay cuts. Struggling businesses lay off workers. As more and more people lose their jobs, the unemployment rate rises. Unemployed workers cannot afford to spend a lot of money, so they will not buy new products. Likewise, workers who are earning less money will try to save money, rather than spend it. As a result, demand for products decreases.

People may wait to make purchases, even when they can afford them. This is often because they believe that prices will continue to drop. Say, for example, that you want to buy a car that costs $15,000. But you know that prices have been going

Consumers may delay major purchases, such as new automobiles, during an economic decline. Potential buyers may also have difficulty obtaining loans, as banks are unwilling to risk lending money.

down. You may decide to wait a month or two and see if the price will drop to $14,000. If a lot of people delay buying cars, it will hurt car dealerships. It will also impact automobile manufacturers. At the same time, people will put off other major purchases that will hurt other businesses. These businesses—and the whole economy—will not recover until people begin spending money again.

Marking Down the Price

Deflation is quite rare. As a rule, prices tend to rise slowly and steadily. They do not usually fall for a prolonged period. This situation, in which prices go up, is called inflation. Inflation is the opposite of deflation. The rate of inflation is measured in percentages. If the annual rate of inflation is 3 percent, the average level of prices is 3 percent higher than it was the previous year. This does not mean that everything gets more expensive. Some items may increase in price and others may decrease. On average, however, overall prices increase during a period of inflation. The value of assets, such as real estate or stocks, also rises due to inflation. Ideally, wages rise at about the same rate as inflation, making the price increases less painful and more affordable.

When the rate of inflation falls, the result is disinflation. Disinflation and deflation are different. When disinflation occurs, inflation is still in effect. The rate of inflation may be 4 percent one year and only 3 percent the next. This is an example of disinflation. Prices are still rising, but they are not rising as quickly.

Economists agree that deflation is bad for the economy. But there are drawbacks to inflation as well. When inflation occurs, goods and services cost slightly more each year. The purchasing power of money declines. Unless people's income also rises, they are able to buy less with their earnings every year. For workers, it is important that their incomes increase along with the rate of inflation.

The Life Cycle of Deflation

Deflation is generally linked to other problems in the economy. In order to understand the role of deflation in economics, it helps to know about the business cycle. The business cycle traces economic growth and contraction (shrinkage). Contraction is negative economic growth. There are four phases to the business cycle: peak, recession, trough, and expansion. The peak is the highest point in economic growth. A recession is a period of slowdown in growth or economic decline. After the downturn, the cycle reaches the trough. This is the lowest point in economic growth (often negative growth or contraction). It is followed by a recovery.

Where does deflation fit into the business cycle? Economists generally worry about the possibility of deflation during recessions. During a recession, unemployment rises. Industrial production falls. Businesses make less money. Consumers cut back on spending. The economy stops growing and expanding as a result.

During a recession, the economic situation usually does not become so bad that deflation occurs. But when deflation does happen, it makes the recession worse. Deflation can make a recession last longer. It can also make the economic effects of the recession more severe. A deflationary spiral is a symptom of a serious economic crisis.

During the Great Depression, bank failures contributed to the economic catastrophe. Customers lost confidence in banks and took their money out of their accounts, which further undermined banks.

An exceptionally deep recession is called a depression. Many economists use the term primarily when referring to the Great Depression, which lasted from 1929 through the early 1940s. During the Great Depression, a deflationary

14

spiral contributed to the over-whelming economic difficulties. Overall, prices declined about 25 percent by the end of the Great Depression.

A period of deflation generally results from the supply of goods being greater than the demand for them. This means that people aren't buying, and merchandise is piling up in stores and warehouses. The specific circumstances vary. This lack of consumer spending may be caused by the government reducing the money supply (often through higher interest rates, which make borrowing money more expensive). Or it may be initiated by the collapse of an asset bubble. An asset bubble occurs when the value of something (like real estate or stocks) is inflated because of high demand. When demand suddenly falls, the value of the assets decreases dramatically and quickly. This in turn reduces the money supply because people aren't investing their money in these assets anymore. When buying or investing decreases, less money is circulating throughout the economy. Prices fall in an attempt to generate demand. Deflation sets in.

MYTHS and FACTS

MYTH A depression and a period of deflation are the same thing.

FACT A depression is a very serious economic downturn. Usually, the term is used to refer to the Great Depression that occurred between 1929 and 1934. Deflation is a sustained drop in price levels. Severe deflation was one factor in the Great Depression, but deflation and economic depression are not always linked.

MYTH When prices for some goods and services dip, the economy has entered a period of deflation.

FACT Price swings in specific goods and services are part of a normal fluctuation in supply and demand. Deflation requires a trend of falling prices across a broad range of goods and services, not just a few sectors, for a sustained period of time.

MYTH The president and Congress are in charge of monitoring and controlling inflation and deflation.

FACT Monetary policy is decided by the Federal Reserve, the central bank of the United States. It is an independent government agency. The president appoints the chairperson of the Federal Reserve. The chairperson submits a report to Congress twice a year. Congress and the president do not have any authority over decisions made by the Federal Reserve, and the Federal Reserve does not get its funding from Congress. The president and Congress do determine fiscal policy, however, which can impact the inflation rate.

CHAPTER TWO
The Mechanisms of Deflation

During uncertain economic times, experts frequently disagree about what the future holds. They might debate what will come next: inflation or deflation. This is not easy to predict. Some economic indicators might point to deflation. One example of this kind of indicator would be declining values in real estate combined with declining prices of everyday items, such as food and clothing. At the same time, other economic indicators might show a return of inflation. For example, the cost of gasoline and health care services may be steadily rising.

When experts disagree, it is difficult to prepare an economic strategy. Should the government expect inflation or deflation? Policy makers must decide which advice to follow. Ordinary Americans are affected by economic uncertainty, too. During economic downturns, they worry about paying bills and losing jobs. The prospect of deflation means that hard economic times could last longer. This fear and uncertainty tends to make people cut their spending, which can worsen deflation or even contribute to a deflationary spiral.

The Role of Supply and Demand

In economics, supply and demand are market forces. The laws of supply and demand examine how goods and services are exchanged in the market. The market is made up of buyers and sellers. Supply is an amount of a good or service that sellers offer for sale at a given price. Demand is the amount of a good or service that buyers will buy at a given price.

Supply and demand explain why prices go up and down, but it involves much more than that. Levels of supply and demand affect interest rates and financial markets. Supply and demand also determine why workers in some types of jobs

Customers in New York City wait for their chance to purchase the first iPhone. Initially more than $500, the price of the iPhone has since fallen dramatically.

have higher salaries than workers in other jobs. There is a greater demand for workers—and the products or services they create—in certain fields.

Supply and demand also affect inflation and deflation. This is because inflation and deflation are dependent on the money supply. Just like there is supply and demand for goods and services, there is supply and demand for money.

When the money supply decreases, money becomes more valuable. The demand for money increases. This means that people want to hold onto their money and save it, rather than spend it. Banks want to sit on their cash reserves and not make loans. Investors and businesses decide to put off potentially risky investments or huge expenditures and save their money till better, more predictable economic times return. As a result of all this, the demand for goods and services decreases. So goods and services become less valuable. As a result, the supply of goods and services goes up. Due to the oversupply of goods and services, the prices go down. When this becomes a sustained (long-lasting) trend, the economy has entered a deflationary period.

Economists generally agree that deflationary periods are damaging to the economy. But some economists argue that there is a beneficial type of deflation. This "good deflation" occurs when industries are able to produce goods more cheaply and efficiently. Therefore, they are able to sell them at lower prices. This often occurs with high-tech products. For example, computers and cell phones were extremely expensive when they were first introduced. Today, however, despite ever-increasing demand, their prices have dropped to far more affordable levels. Good deflation is not accompanied by rising unemployment or other negative economic effects.

Other experts are skeptical of the idea of good deflation. Most examples of good deflation only pertain to one sector of the economy, such as technology. When deflation occurs more broadly throughout the economy, the economy suffers.

What's the Price?

Deflation is defined as an overall drop in prices of goods and services. So how do economists determine whether prices are increasing or decreasing? Economists use price indexes to measure price levels. Price indexes are observations of current prices compared to prices for the same goods and services during some earlier period.

When examining inflation and deflation, economists look at the consumer price index (CPI). It is also known as the cost-of-living index or the retail price index. The CPI measures the prices of the goods and services used by a typical household. This includes four hundred items considered to be a "market basket." The basket includes goods and services necessary for a decent standard of living.

The consumer price index examines the changing prices of goods and services—including entertainment, like movie tickets—that reflect consumer spending.

There are a number of different categories, such as food, medical services, transportation, and entertainment. Each month, some prices rise and others fall. The consumer price index determines the average change over time in overall prices of goods and services. The CPI does not consider assets, such as real estate, life insurance policies, or stocks, even though these assets are subject to inflation and deflation, too. The CPI is restricted to goods and services.

The government and financial institutions use CPI data when making policy decisions. In some labor contracts, salaries are linked to the CPI. Social Security payments, which are collected by retired people, are also tied to the CPI. Therefore, when the cost of living rises, a worker's salary rises. Retirees collect larger Social Security payments. But if deflation were to occur, these salaries and payments would be reduced.

The government also considers the CPI when determining monetary policy. If there are drastic changes in the index, the government will take steps to stabilize prices. The Federal Reserve may raise or lower interest rates, decreasing or increasing the money supply as needed.

Managing Deflation

The government has two primary instruments in managing the economy: fiscal policy and monetary policy. Fiscal policy concerns the nation's budget. It deals with tax rates and government spending. One of the goals of fiscal policy is to keep unemployment levels low. Other goals include price stability and economic growth. Therefore, some decisions on fiscal policy can affect the rate of inflation. Fiscal policy is controlled by the president and Congress.

Monetary policy, rather than fiscal policy, however, is the most important tool in controlling inflation and deflation.

The Federal Reserve Board Building in Washington, D.C., contains the offices of the Fed's Board of Governors. The Federal Reserve is responsible for the nation's monetary policy.

Monetary policy is determined by the Federal Reserve System, which acts as the central bank in the United States. All U.S. banks and financial institutions must comply with Federal Reserve regulations. Monetary policy concerns the money supply. One of the most important jobs of the Federal Reserve System (often called the Fed) is controlling the amount of money in circulation. When the Federal Reserve aims to reduce inflationary pressures, it restricts the money supply (pulls money out of circulation, often through higher interest rates). When the Federal Reserve aims to avert recession—and possible deflation—it increases the money supply (injects money into circulation, often through lower interest rates). In this way, the Federal Reserve manipulates supply and demand of money.

The supply and demand of money also determines the interest rate. Interest is a percentage of the original loan amount you must pay as a fee for borrowing money. If you buy a house or a car, you want a low interest rate. That means that you will pay less interest as you repay your loan. If you make an investment that pays a certain amount of interest to you, however, you want a high interest rate. This means that you will earn more money from the interest earned on your initial investment. When the Federal Reserve restricts the money supply, less money is available for loans. Interest rates increase. When the Fed increases the money supply, more money is available for loans. Interest rates decrease.

Deflation and the Great Depression

The Great Depression was the most severe economic crisis in modern history. It was not just an economic catastrophe. It was also a time of political and social upheaval. People in the United States had never before experienced such financial hardship.

Deflation was one important and devastating feature of the Great Depression. It was the worst period of deflation ever to occur in the United States. Deflation itself did not cause the depression. But deflation made the economic crisis even worse.

So what led to the Great Depression and the deflation that occurred during this time? Many factors contributed to the initial economic downturn. There is much debate over the causes. In general, economists agree that the Federal Reserve

During the Great Depression, poverty-stricken Americans—especially unemployed men—populated shantytowns that arose near major cities. Here, shacks dot the waterfront of Seattle in 1933.

made mistakes in handling monetary policy before and during the Great Depression. Some economists claim that a decline in the money supply was a key contributing factor. The resulting economic crisis began in the United States and spread across the world.

In the decade leading up to the Great Depression, Americans enjoyed a period of economic prosperity. The decade is sometimes called the Roaring Twenties, for both its raucous high society spirit and its freewheeling, largely unregulated, business-friendly economy. World War I had ended in 1918, and, while Europe struggled to recover, the United States became the richest and most powerful nation in the world. Ordinary Americans began buying newly available and affordable luxuries. More and more people got electricity in their homes. They purchased new electric appliances, including radios and telephones.

Most of all, ordinary Americans began buying cars. This supported a growing automobile industry. By the end of the decade, nearly 450,000 people worked for auto and auto parts manufacturers. The auto industry also boosted other sectors, since it required raw materials, such as rubber and steel. Many people were employed in building roads and other infrastructure needed for the increasing number of cars being driven.

In order to pay for their new luxuries, Americans borrowed money. Banks and new financial companies were glad to lend people this money. Interest rates were sometimes very high, however. For a new car, the annual interest rate could be about 30 percent. People went into debt anyway because they were sure that they would be able to pay back the money, given how strong the economy was.

The 1920s were also a period of growth in the stock market. Few Americans owned stock—less than one in ten people (today, almost half of all households are invested in the stock market in some way). But the financial markets were important in deciding interest rates and availability of credit across the nation. Some economists and policy makers began to worry that the stock market was not stable. Investors buying stock were speculating. This means that they were gambling on the likelihood that they would be able to sell for a large profit later. Speculation drove up the price of stocks.

The Federal Reserve was afraid that this speculative investment bubble would suddenly burst and there would be a stock

On October 29, 1929, panicked stockholders sold their shares and the stock market plummeted. The date of the crash is remembered as Black Tuesday.

market crash. In order to discourage speculation, the Federal Reserve tried to choke off the flow of money by raising interest rates in 1928. Less money in circulation would mean that investors had less money to use for risky investments that could go bad and burst the stock market bubble. Overall, this reduction of the money supply hurt the economy. The United States began to slip into a recession. As this occurred, the Federal Reserve took no action to increase the money supply. In late 1929, the stock market crashed, partly as a result of Federal Reserve monetary policies. The Great Crash, as it is sometimes called, impacted the entire economy. One of the results was severe deflation.

CHAPTER THREE

The Effects of Deflation

The economy in the United States has been inflationary for more than fifty years. Today, most people probably can't imagine day-to-day life during a period of deflation. In addition to falling prices, deflation causes general uncertainty and anxiety about the economy. Since unemployment is higher during deflationary periods, even people who are still employed worry about their jobs. Prices are lower, but wages are also lower. Therefore, people do not spend a lot of money on luxuries and large purchases. People also delay big purchases in the hope that the trend of falling prices might continue and they can get a good bargain.

This caution is reasonable, since deflation tends to occur during economic downturns. But consumer spending helps drive the economy. When people are careful about their spending, economic growth slows. This sets in motion a vicious cycle—unsold goods, lower production, still lower prices, lower profits, layoffs, and even more reduced consumer spending. In this way, deflation can prolong a recession.

Impact on Individuals

Consumers ordinarily welcome lower prices for goods and services. But deflation generally accompanies an economic downturn. This often means that people have less money to spend. They are more careful about how they spend their money. When consumers are cautious about spending, businesses make less money. They may lower workers' pay. Sometimes, they are forced to lay off workers.

Unemployment levels rise during a period of deflation. When someone loses his or her job, it hurts the entire household. The friends, neighbors, and family members of unemployed workers start worrying more about whether their own jobs are secure. This can lower consumer demand for goods and services as people hunker down and save money in case of lean times ahead. People delay major purchases. Some people cannot afford major purchases. Other people wait to see if prices will drop further.

Factors such as falling prices, decreased demand, and rising unemployment can potentially cause a deflationary spiral. This is the worst-case scenario for deflation. In a deflationary spiral, the different effects of deflation make the overall trend worse. It can become a vicious and negative cycle. Falling prices, for example, cause lower profits for businesses which, in turn, result in higher unemployment. Higher employment leads to less spending. Reduced consumer spending brings about a lower demand for goods. Decreased demand causes an oversupply of goods. Therefore, businesses reduce prices. Their profits get even smaller, and they lay off even more workers. The whole cycle continues and deepens in a downward spiral.

During a recession, even highly qualified workers can have difficulty finding a new job. In recent downturns, people have been unemployed an average of six months or more.

Other factors also contribute to the woes of deflation for individuals. Deflation makes it harder for people to pay off loans. The value of money increases during a period of deflation. Therefore, the value of debt also increases. Even though the value of debt is greater, people still have to meet fixed monthly payments. Because of deflation, these fixed payments now represent a greater share of their purchasing power. Making monthly payments of $200 on a car loan is a lot harder during a deflationary period because you are making less money each paycheck and have less to spend.

Rising unemployment and lower wages add to people's difficulties in repaying debt. Also, the asset bought with the loan may decline in value, even as the value of the loan increases. During a deflationary period, a home bought with the help of a loan may end up being worth less than you paid for it, even though the value—the actual cost—of that loan increases.

During a deflationary period, people are sometimes unable to come up with the money needed to repay loans. This hurts individual debtors as well as the financial institutions that hold the loans. Deflation also makes it more difficult for people to obtain new loans. Banks and other lenders are less likely to issue loans during tough economic times. As a result, people who

A house in Altadena is among 1,500 homes in southern California listed at an eleven-day foreclosure auction. During a recession, foreclosure rates can soar as borrowers fall behind on their payments.

want to buy a new car or start a new business may not be able to do so. This is harmful for individuals, businesses, and the overall economy.

Sometimes, people are forced to take extreme measures to raise money, whether it is needed for loan payments or just day-to-day expenses. They may begin to sell off assets, such as real estate, stocks, or retirement investments. They may even have to sell their homes. If they can't repay their home loan payments, the bank who owns their mortgage (a loan to help buy a home) will seize it and force them out. This is known as foreclosure.

During an economic downturn, they will not receive good prices for these assets. In addition, if many people sell assets at the same time, overall market prices for the assets will fall. No one will receive a good return on their investments or raise as much cash as they may need.

Impact on Businesses and Banks

For businesses, decreasing prices lead to lower profits. Decreased consumer demand means that fewer goods and services are being sold. Lower demand causes an oversupply of goods to accumulate. This harms both the businesses that sell goods and services and the manufacturers that produce the goods.

During a period of deflation, businesses adopt money-saving policies in an attempt to remain profitable. Sometimes, businesses struggle just to survive. This impacts workers who may take pay cuts to save their jobs. Layoffs may occur. Factories may temporarily halt production due to a lack of consumer demand. Workers are left without pay during the stretches that factories are shut down.

The Federal Reserve and Your Bank

The Federal Reserve was established in 1913 as the central bank of the United States. The central bank is responsible for a nation's financial policies.

The Federal Reserve's primary job is overseeing the nation's money supply. It also has other functions. It clears checks, for example. If you write a check, it goes through a Federal Reserve bank as part of the transaction. It supervises and regulates banks. It even acts as the banker for the federal government: The U.S. Treasury deposits money in Federal Reserve bank accounts. The money is used for Social Security payments, tax refunds, and other expenses. The Federal Reserve also circulates currency and withdraws old coins and banknotes.

The precise duties and roles of the Federal Reserve are often modified. For example, since 1933, the Federal Reserve has worked in cooperation with the Federal Deposit Insurance Corporation (FDIC). The FDIC was established during the Great Depression as a response to runs on banks (when nervous depositors withdraw all their money) and bank collapses. The FDIC insures deposits in banks. If a bank fails, people do not lose their money (or at least not all of it). Therefore, during an economic downturn, the financial system is no longer further stressed by panicked consumers taking their money out of banks and causing them to shut down, as they were before the creation of the FDIC. When banks fail and close, the economy loses some of the energy required to sustain it. This is why banks must be protected—and protect themselves—from failure at all costs.

35

Businesses do not make major investments in equipment, facilities, or the research and development of new products during difficult economic times. One reason is that the value of money increases due to deflation. Businesses may hoard money instead of risking it on investments that seem to be losing value. Instead, they will wait for a more favorable economic climate. When many businesses postpone investing, however, it slows the growth of the economy. It can also hurt individual businesses. If a company decides to cut research and development of new products, for example, it will fail to attract new customers or get existing customers excited about something new. As a result, its growth will slow and its profitability will slip further.

Even when they take drastic cost-cutting measures, businesses are not always able to survive. Some companies go bankrupt. Bankruptcy occurs when an individual or company cannot pay its debts. A business is sometimes able to reopen after declaring bankruptcy. In other cases, the business closes permanently.

Businesses, like individuals, have a tougher time repaying their debts during a period of deflation. This causes financial hardship for businesses. It also impacts banks and other lenders. Banks experience difficulty when they are unable to collect loan

A Circuit City store in New York City advertises steep sales. The company, once the nation's second-largest electronics retailer, declared bankruptcy and closed all of its stores in 2009.

payments. They are also hurt by bankruptcies of companies to which they have lent money. Banks take hold of a company's assets when the business goes bankrupt. But these assets are often of less value than the price of the original loan.

After experiencing billions of dollars in losses, the investment bank Merrill Lynch was taken over by Bank of America. Here, the two CEOs shake hands on the deal.

During hard economic times, the bank is often unable to sell these seized assets for a profit. If the bank sells the assets anyway and takes a loss, it adds to the oversupply of assets on the market. The increasing oversupply can further contribute to a deflationary spiral. Prices fall further due to supply outstripping demand. This stresses businesses and increases the likelihood of further defaults on loans and bankruptcies.

In the worst cases, this can cause banks to collapse. The most vulnerable banks are the ones that made risky loans. For example, banks may grant loans to people or businesses that are unlikely to be able to repay them. When the economy falters, these companies default on their loans, and the bank loses money. The money that the bank loses is the deposits of ordinary people who have checking and savings accounts with the bank. Luckily, most deposits are insured by the federal government, but only up to $250,000. If someone has more than that amount deposited with a bank that fails, he or she may lose the balance of those savings.

Most banks are not in danger of failure during a period of deflation. But they are less likely to grant loans. Banks may not have as much money to offer due to losses on investments (which decrease in value during a deflationary period) and loan defaults. They are more likely to be cautious during an economic downturn as well. Banks want to be sure that debtors will be able to pay back the money they borrow. And banks will make more of a profit during a healthy economic climate when interest rates are higher. During times of deflation, the Federal Reserve lowers interest rates, which means lenders do not have to pay as much to the bank when repaying a loan.

CHAPTER FOUR
Fighting Deflation

For the United States, deflation has mostly been a phenomenon of the past. Still, this does not mean that economic policy makers should discount the future possibility of deflation. A future period of deflation may be unlikely to occur, but it is not completely impossible. Effective monetary policy can avert deflation during economic downturns. Preventing deflation is a far preferable option to reversing deflation and the negative ripple effects associated with it once they take hold.

If early signs of deflation begin to appear, the government takes immediate action to stabilize prices. Policy makers use monetary policy to oppose deflation directly. Monetary policy involves the money supply, which should be increased to help fight off deflation. Basically, money needs to be injected into circulation and cash put in consumers' and businesses' hands. Monetary policy is determined by the Federal Reserve.

During a recession, the government may also enact fiscal policy intended to stabilize the economy. Congress and the

41

president decide fiscal policy. Fiscal policy does not influence the money supply. But fiscal measures can reduce unemployment and increase demand for goods and services. This will increase consumer spending, which will help stabilize prices and keep

Fannie Mae—the Federal National Mortgage Association—holds or guarantees many of the mortgages in the United States.

money circulating throughout the economy. Good fiscal policy can shorten a recession and minimize its economic impact.

Tools and Strategies for Combating Deflation

In the News

There is no one-size-fits-all approach to fighting deflation. Every economic crisis is unique. During every economic decline, there are various specific factors that sparked the downturn. Policy makers must examine the situation and take action to bolster the most vulnerable parts of the economy.

Moreover, because the Federal Reserve has been successful in preventing deflation, it has not occurred in the United States in many decades. Therefore, any discussion of how the American government would deal with deflation is speculative. If deflation really did become entrenched, it would be a new phenomenon in the modern American economy. Some approaches toward reversing deflation would probably be successful. Others might

43

be less effective. The government would have to adapt its policies depending on which measures worked the best.

At the earliest sign that deflationary pressures are building, the Federal Reserve usually lowers interest rates, thereby increasing the money supply. When interest rates are low, it costs less to borrow money. This encourages people to take out loans and spend money. If interest rates were to approach zero, however (meaning the borrower would not have to pay any interest on the loan, only repay the loan itself), the Federal Reserve could not lower the rates any further. This would halt the Federal Reserve's ability to counter deflation by adjusting interest rates.

During a recession, the federal government uses fiscal policy to influence the economy. Government spending can help bring the economy back to life. Congress and the president might authorize projects, such as building new roads or improving the facilities, supplies, and equipment used in public schools. This will provide jobs for the unemployed. It will increase demand for goods and services. Money from these projects— and from the paychecks they provide—begins to circulate through the economy.

Another option that the government can use to spur the economy and increase the amount of money circulating throughout the economy is to cut taxes. If businesses and individuals pay less in taxes, they have more money to spend. However, this is effective only if people spend the money, rather than save it. If the economic downturn is serious enough, many businesses and individuals become cautious about spending and prefer to sit on cash until better and more secure times return. They want to set something aside should the bad times continue or get even worse. They are afraid of losing what little they may have left, so they cling to their cash reserves.

These U.S. Treasury checks are tax rebate checks that were sent out to many Americans in an effort to prevent a recession. This is an example of fiscal stimulus.

Signs of Recovery

During an economic downturn, people are constantly asking when the economy will improve. Usually, there is no clear

Commuters pass through New York City's bustling Grand Central Terminal during morning rush hour. A decrease in the unemployment rate is a healthy sign of an economy recovering from a recession.

turning point. Economic indicators may improve for a month or two, then fall back. It can be a "two steps forward, one step back" situation. Though there is general progress toward improvement, economic recovery is a gradual and sometimes halting process.

Even when the chairman of the Federal Reserve announces that a recession is over, it will take time for ordinary people to regain confidence in the economy and begin spending again and for companies to resume hiring.

Experts examine certain economic indicators to determine whether the economy is improving. Manufacturers will report new orders for goods. Stock market indexes will rise. Fewer people will file for unemployment benefits—this shows that fewer people are losing jobs. Companies, instead of announcing a new round of layoffs, will instead report the hiring of first temporary and then permanent full-time employees. As the recovery progresses, industrial production will rise. The economy will begin to grow. There will be setbacks during an economic recovery, but overall, these economic indicators will show growth.

It can take months before economists can state for certain that a healthy recovery is underway. Part of this is because of the time it takes to process economic data. There is no way of determining the health of the economy until all of the relevant economic reports are released. Another reason is that some areas of the economy improve more quickly than others. Unemployment rates, for example, do not begin to fall until the economy is well into the recovery process, not just in the early stages. Employers do not begin to hire new workers until they are confident that their business is solid. Lending—and therefore spending—also takes time to recover.

How do inflation and deflation figure in an economic recovery? Experts often disagree on whether various indicators predict inflation or deflation. Economists are more likely to worry about deflation in the midst of an economic downturn. Therefore, the government takes steps to avert deflation. The money supply is increased. Economic stimulus measures are enacted. During an economic recovery, however, an increased money supply could trigger inflation.

The Federal Reserve has to act with great care in order to maintain price stability and prevent the influx of too much money into the economy. If there is too much cash in circulation and goods and services are in short supply after a recession, prices will shoot up and already nervous consumers will feel pinched. Yet if the Fed exerts too tight a control on the money supply and holds back the flow of cash, an already fragile economic recovery may be choked off and deflation will return. The Federal Reserve must achieve a delicate balancing act and not take any drastic actions either way regarding the lowering or raising of interest rates that could cause the economy to falter.

Overcoming the Great Depression

The Great Depression deepened after the 1929 stock market crash. The government was slow to intervene in the economy. This was standard policy for the times. Most economists believed that the economy was largely self-regulating. They thought that the value of stocks, real estate, and other assets would be automatically readjusted during the downturn. The economy would hit bottom, then investment would resume. Financially sound business enterprises would survive the depression. Others would fail. But the Great Depression defied all of their expectations of recovery.

When banks began to collapse, the government did nothing. Economists believed that only weak banks would fail. Healthy banks would weather the depression. Instead, bank failures increased. Half of all the banks in the country collapsed or merged with other banks. People rushed to the bank to take out their money in fear that their bank would fail too. Surviving banks stopped issuing loans and access to cash was essentially frozen. The entire banking system reached a crisis, and the circulation of money was halted. Because banks are a source of money, these grim developments decreased the money supply. This contributed to deflation, helping to tip a bad economic recession into a very grave depression.

The Federal Reserve did not take adequate action to combat deflation. It did not increase the money supply until 1932, when interest rates were finally lowered. Prices began to stabilize. But later in 1932, the Federal Reserve reversed this policy, and the economy went into decline again. Deflation

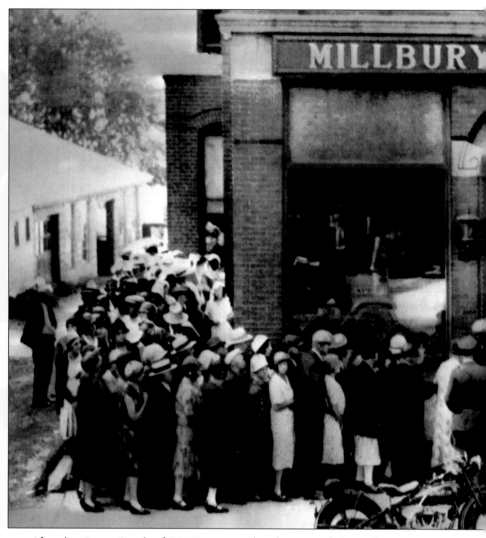

After the Great Crash of 1929, a crowd rushes to withdraw their money from the local bank.

was actually worse in 1932 than during any other year of the Great Depression.

When Franklin Delano Roosevelt became president in 1933, his administration took drastic action to repair the

economy. This included both monetary and fiscal measures. Roosevelt launched a huge array of projects and programs that would give people work, protect their savings, develop America's infrastructure, and revive the economy. This enormous undertaking was called the New Deal.

Two days after taking office, Roosevelt shut down the nation's banks. During this "bank holiday," he gave the Federal Reserve and other agencies new powers to regulate and support the banks. Three days later, banks began opening again.

The economy slowly began to improve. The Federal Reserve increased the money supply and helped strengthen American banks. Banks started issuing more loans. More businesses and individuals were willing and able to take out loans. As a result, investment increased, creating more spending by businesses and additional jobs.

The New Deal authorized many work relief programs. Unemployed people were given public jobs by the government. They built bridges, hospitals, and schools. They planted

51

Men in Arkansas work on a flood control project in 1939. Part of the New Deal, the Works Progress Administration (WPA) provided jobs for unemployed workers during the Great Depression.

forests, installed electric lines, and completed many other projects. There were even jobs created for unemployed actors, artists, photographers, and writers. The goal of the work relief programs was to aid the unemployed and spur the consumer economy. These newly reemployed workers would now have money to spend. Money returned to the economy would further increase demand for goods and services. As a result, production would increase and still more jobs would be created, leading to even more spending. A positive cycle would take hold and lead to American economic recovery.

Ten Great Questions
to Ask a Financial Adviser

1 Could a prolonged period of deflation or a deflationary spiral happen again in the United States?

2 How does deflation begin?

3 How can I protect my savings and investments during a period of deflation?

4 Are there any investment opportunities I can take advantage of during a period of deflation?

5 Would this be a good time to take out a loan on a large purchase—because of low interest rates—or should I instead use my money to pay back my debts?

6 What financial controls and regulations protect the economy from deflation?

7 Is a period of deflation likely to be sustained or will it end quickly?

8 How do I know that a period of deflation has ended?

9 Is inflation or even hyperinflation likely to occur as the economy emerges from a recession or period of deflation?

10 What are the signs of a financial recovery from a recession?

CHAPTER FIVE

Surviving Deflation

In 2000, the U.S. economy fell into a recession. The high-tech bubble—sometimes called the dot-com boom—suddenly burst. People had invested heavily in information technology and other high-tech stocks and Web retailers. Some of these companies had attracted investors even though they had not yet created any actual products or services. They had merely established a Web presence and were promising to begin selling goods or services soon.

Suddenly, the value of these investments crashed as Web speculation slowed. Investors pulled out after beginning to question the viability of these start-up tech companies that had little or nothing to show for all the money that had been poured into them. Workers lost their jobs. Economic growth slowed. The money supply shrank as consumers, investors, and businesses became conservative with their cash.

In response, beginning in 2001, the Federal Reserve began lowering interest rates. In early 2003, a statement issued by the

The telecom giant WorldCom filed for bankruptcy, brought down by corporate fraud. Former CEO Bernard Ebbers, shown here entering a courthouse, was sentenced to twenty-five years in prison for his role in the corporate crimes.

Federal Reserve warned that an "unwelcome fall in inflation" could occur if economic activity didn't pick up and people and companies didn't begin spending again. Shortly afterward, Alan Greenspan, then chairman of the Federal Reserve, mentioned the possibility of deflation. The Federal Reserve continued lowering interest rates to prevent that. By summer of 2003, the interest rate stood at only 1 percent. This was the lowest level since 1958.

By the end of 2003, the economy was rebounding. Investment and employment rates increased. Economic growth resumed. Throughout the recession, following the Fed's initial lowering of interest rates, the struggling economy had been propped up by consumer spending. People were attracted by the low interest rates and took out loans. They bought new homes and cars. Fears of deflation disappeared.

This episode demonstrates lessons learned from the Great Depression. Economists did not forget the damage done by deflation in the early years of that crisis. This time, the Federal Reserve took quick action to prevent any possibility of that kind of devastating deflation taking hold and creating a downward economic spiral that would take years to pull out of. Also, the financial system today is much better regulated. After the Great Depression, many reforms were put into place. Economists and lawmakers wanted to prevent any chance that a crisis like the Great Depression could ever happen again.

Deflation and the "Depression Mentality"

Some people who lived through the Great Depression acquired what is sometimes called the "depression mentality." Their experiences during those years of extreme hardship left them feeling insecure about money. Even if they are now wealthy and the current economy is healthy, they still worry about the possibility of losing all their money.

This mind-set is due partly to the effects of deflation during the Great Depression. People who lived through the depression sometimes hoard money even today. As a result of deflation during that crisis, money was scarce. Even though the price of goods and services sank, people still didn't have enough money to be able to afford them. People learned to hang onto money instead of spending it on something that might be even cheaper tomorrow, investing it in a business that might go bust, or even putting it in a bank that might fail at any time.

People who lived through the depression may also tend to avoid financial risk. They may avoid investing money for fear that the company they invest in may go

Modern technology makes managing money—and running up debt—easy to do, but many people who survived economic hardship take old-fashioned care with their money.

bankrupt, taking their savings with them. They may even refuse to use credit cards or take out loans. During the depression, banks folded, businesses closed, and the stock market crashed. These experiences left many people distrustful of financial institutions. Also, deflation caused the real value of loans to increase while wages decreased. As a result, some depression-era survivors, no matter how wealthy in later life, became wary of putting themselves into debt in case something happened that would prevent them from paying it back.

Prolonged economic crises can be traumatic, especially when people lose their businesses, home, land, jobs, or savings. Even if they recover financially, they may never recover emotionally. Their future money decisions will always be haunted and informed by their fear of a new economic catastrophe.

Lessons Learned from the Great Depression

During economic downturns, people often make comparisons to the Great Depression. In truth, though, the Great Depression

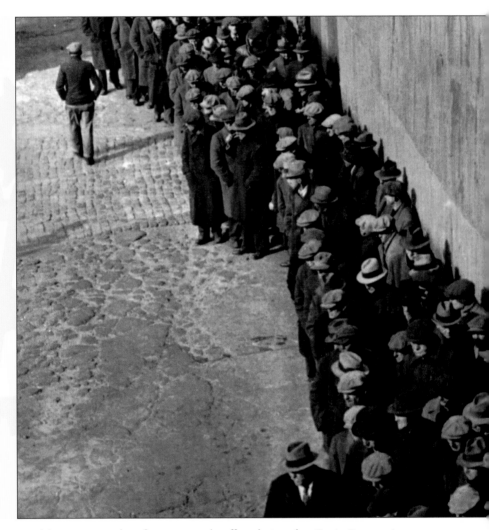

Men wait in a line for soup and coffee during the Great Depression. Many people were forced to turn to community organizations, churches, and government programs for aid.

was unique. No other financial crisis has wreaked such devastation or caused such hardship and turmoil as did the Great Depression, both across America and worldwide.

Today, people fear losing their jobs, homes, or savings during a recession. Back then, many people worried not only about those things but also about even more basic human needs—like finding ways to keep their families fed, sheltered, and healthy enough to stay alive. Also, the government did not then provide safety nets, such as unemployment benefits or food stamps. During the Great Depression, people ran out of money for buying food and paying bills. Farmers lost their land and equipment. Homeless people camped out in Hoovervilles set up outside cities (named after U.S. president Herbert Hoover whose inaction in the early years of the economic crisis helped deepen and lengthen it). Workers watched factories close their doors and padlock their gates. People lined up to receive free bread or soup.

Statistics relating to the Great Depression confirm the scale of the crisis. The first major warning signal of the coming depression was the stock market crash. The peak of the Dow Jones Industrial Average—an important stock market index—reached 386.10 in September 1929. By July 1930, it had plunged to its lowest point of 41.22. In the wake of the crash, thousands of banks failed—more than 20 percent of the banks in the country. The real gross domestic product (GDP)—the value of all goods and services produced in the country—declined by about 30 percent from 1929 to 1933. Rates of exports, industrial production, and investment all fell. In 1929, before the stock market crash, the unemployment rate stood at just over 3 percent. By 1933, 25 percent of all Americans were unemployed.

Depression-era statistics related to deflation and the money supply are particularly revealing. In 1930, the inflation rate was about -4 percent. In 1931, it fell to -10 percent. In 1932, in the depths of the economic crisis, it reached -11.38 percent. In 1933, when the very slow recovery from the depression began, the inflation rate rose to about

-3 percent. In total, the rate of deflation between 1929 and 1933 was higher than 25 percent.

Deflation affected the real interest rates (the cost of borrowing when deflation and the resulting increase in the value of

In March 1933, President Franklin Roosevelt signed the Emergency Banking Act to deal with the banking crisis. A few months later, the Banking Act introduced broader reform to the economic system.

money are factored in). The nominal interest rates set by the Federal Reserve stood at 3.56 percent in 1930. The Federal Reserve eventually lowered it to under 3 percent. Nonetheless, the real interest rates reached about 15 percent during 1931 and 1932. With such high real interest rates, few people and businesses dared to take out loans.

Changes in the money supply reflected the same trends. The money supply increased up until 1929 when the stock market crashed. From 1929 until 1933, it declined as investors withdrew from the market, banks failed, jobs evaporated, and consumers tried to save what little money they still had. From 1933 onward, as recovery began to take hold and Roosevelt's New Deal injected cash, investments, and jobs back into the economy, the money supply increased once again. Many economists point to the decreased money supply as the major cause of deflation during the Great Depression.

Under Roosevelt, the government acted to reverse the economic crisis. It also took steps to ensure that such a situation could never occur again. New banking and financial regulations were enacted. The Federal Reserve was strengthened. Today, some economics textbooks state that the chairperson of the Federal Reserve is the most important person in the United States other than the president. This is because of the Federal Reserve's role in managing the economy.

In addition, the Great Depression introduced a new era in economic theory. Economists developed new ideas about how employment rates, prices, and production levels relate to the business cycle. In part, this was a reaction to the Great Depression. Economists wanted to solve the problem of how to prevent another similarly severe economic calamity.

Could Deflation Occur Again?

During every economic downturn, experts debate what trends to expect next. When will the stock market rebound? What will the latest unemployment figures indicate? Are orders for manufactured goods on the upswing? Is consumer confidence down along with spending?

The rate of inflation is an important indicator. What should people expect in the coming months, inflation or deflation? When the economy is experiencing uncertain times, experts do not agree on the answer. Economists often interpret the same economic data differently. Some economists examine the facts and statistics and conclude that inflation will occur. Others look at the same information and predict an episode of deflation. Then again, some economists believe that over the long term, inflation will always dominate. Others insist that sustained deflation will eventually arrive as part of the low ebb of the business cycle. This viewpoint is in the minority, however. Most economists do not see it as a normal part of the business cycle, but as an extraordinary and abnormal phenomenon that can and should be prevented at all costs.

The Federal Reserve tends to support a moderate rate of inflation. If inflation is controlled at about 2 percent, there will be little chance that the economy would experience deflation. A moderate rate of inflation will not hurt consumers. When prices only increase by 2 percent every year, people will still be able to afford a decent standard of living. The second half of the twentieth century and the beginning of the twenty-first were characterized by a sustained period of mostly moderate inflation (except for a period in the late 1970s when the inflation rate was in the double digits). This was a result of sustained economic growth. But it was also due, in part, to wise and effective government economic policy.

The American Recovery and Reinvestment Act of 2009 was enacted to stimulate the economy, which had been battered by the recession. It included generous provisions for renewable energy.

So, could deflation occur again? There is no easy answer. The field of economics is an extraordinarily complex subject. It is impossible to predict economic trends with perfect accuracy. Economists also have to keep up with new developments in the

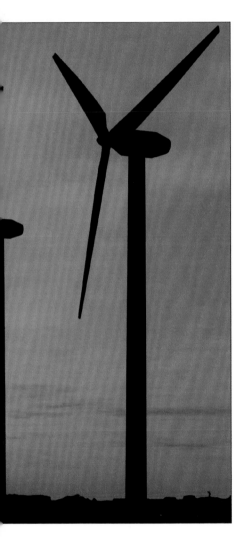

world economy. Technological advances can bring about unexpected changes. Economies in different countries often shift and impact other economies. Political events, natural catastrophes, social trends, and many other factors can affect national economies or the world economy in unexpected ways.

Nevertheless, it is unlikely that an economic downturn could lead to the drastic period of deflation seen during the Great Depression. Those levels of deflation were unusually high, and, initially, the government did little to counteract the shrinking money supply and stimulate the economy. Back then, deflation occurred for a sustained length of time—years, not merely months. Today, economic policies and controls are far more sophisticated than they were during the Great Depression. The government would act quickly and would probably be able to rein in deflation before it caused a deflationary spiral.

This doesn't mean that the United States will never again experience deflation. It is possible that deflation could occur as a symptom of an economic recession. But if this did happen, the rate of deflation would probably not reach critical levels. The government would probably take decisive action in order to minimize the length of the period of deflation. Deflation is considered such a potentially dangerous economic condition that the government will do its best to prevent its recurrence. In so doing, it will always endeavor to safeguard America from prolonged economic harm, keep American businesses and industries humming, provide ample investment opportunities, protect its citizens' earnings and savings and homes, and keep Americans working. By preventing and fighting deflation, the federal government helps ensure our continued access to an affordable standard of living. In this way, it is helping to pre- serve the American Dream.

GLOSSARY

bankruptcy The legal process in which a person or group declares inability to pay off debts.

business cycle Normal alternating periods of growth and contraction in the economy.

central bank An institution or agency, either associated with the government or independent, that is responsible for exercising control of a nation's monetary and financial systems.

currency Something that is used as a medium of exchange; paper and coin money.

debt Something that is owed or that one is bound to pay or perform for another person.

deflation A sustained drop in general price levels of goods and services.

demand The amount of a good or service that buyers will purchase at a given price.

depression A prolonged economic downturn (or trough in the business cycle) marked by high unemployment levels.

disinflation A slowing of the increase in the rate of inflation.

fiscal policy The use of government spending and taxing powers to influence economic activity.

gross domestic product (GDP) The value of all the goods and services produced in a nation during a period of time, usually a year.

hyperinflation An rapid and extreme rise in inflation.

inflation An increase in general price levels of goods and services.

interest A sum paid or charged for the use of money or for borrowing money; often expressed as a percentage of money borrowed and to be paid back within a given time.

monetary policy Actions taken by the Federal Reserve to regulate inflation levels and economic activity by increasing or decreasing interest rates and the money supply.

money supply Money in the economy that can be exchanged for goods and services.

profit The money left to a producer or employer from income after costs such as wages, rent, and raw materials are paid.

recession An economic downturn in the business cycle, usually defined as six months or more of declining GDP.

recovery The upward phase of the business cycle in which economic conditions improve.

stock Ownership shares of a company or corporation.

supply An amount of a good or service that sellers offer for sale at a given price.

wages A worker's payment for labor services, often on an hourly, daily, or weekly basis.

FOR MORE INFORMATION

Bank of Canada
234 Wellington Street
Ottawa, ON K1A 0G9
Canada
(800) 303-1282
Web site: http://www.bankofcanada.ca
This is the central bank of Canada.

Board of Governors of the Federal Reserve System
20th Street and Constitution Avenue NW
Washington, DC 20551
Web site: http://www.federalreserve.gov
This is the central bank of the United States.

Department of Finance Canada
140 O'Connor Street
Ottawa, ON K1A 0G5
Canada
(613) 992-1573
Web site: http://www.fin.gc.ca
This department oversees Canada's budget and spending.

Federal Deposit Insurance Corporation (FDIC)
Public Information Center

3501 North Fairfax Drive
Arlington, VA 22226
(877) 275-3342
Web site: http://www.fdic.gov
This government agency insures bank deposits.

National Economists Club
P.O. Box 19281
Washington, DC 20036
(703) 493-8824
Web site: http://www.national-economists.org
The goal of this nonprofit, nonpartisan organization is
    to encourage and sponsor discussion and an exchange
    of ideas on economic trends and issues relevant
    public policy.

U.S. Department of the Treasury
1500 Pennsylvania Avenue NW
Washington, DC 20220
(202) 622-2000
Web site: http://www.treas.gov
The Department of the Treasury's mission is to serve the
    American people and strengthen national security by
    managing the U.S. government's finances effectively, pro-
    moting economic growth and stability, and ensuring the
    safety, soundness, and security of the U.S. and international
    financial systems.

White House
1600 Pennsylvania Avenue NW

Washington, DC 20500
(202) 456-1414
Web site: http://www.whitehouse.gov
The White House is the official residence of the president
   of the United States. It also contains the offices of the
   president and his or her top staff members. The above
   URL is the official Web site for the White House and the
   president of the United States.

Web Sites

Due to the changing nature of Internet links, Rosen Publishing
has developed an online list of Web sites related to the subject
of this book. This site is updated regularly. Please use this link
to access this list:

http://www.rosenlinks.com/rwe/defl

FOR FURTHER READING

Clifford, Tim. *Our Economy in Action*. Vero Beach, FL: Rourke Publishing, LLC, 2009.

Craats, Rennay. *Economy: USA Past Present Future*. New York, NY: Weigl Publishers, 2009.

Downing, David. *Political and Economic Systems: Capitalism*. Chicago, IL: Heinemann Library, 2008.

Flynn, Sean Masaki. *Economics for Dummies*. Hoboken, NJ: John Wiley & Sons, Inc., 2005.

Gilman, Laura Anne. *Economics* (How Economics Works). Minneapolis, MN: Lerner Publications, 2006.

Hall, Alvin. *Show Me the Money: How to Make Cents of Economics*. New York, NY: DK, 2008.

Hart, Joyce. *How Inflation Works* (Real World Economics). New York, NY: Rosen Publishing Group, 2009.

Landau, Elaine. *The Great Depression*. New York, NY: Children's Press, 2006.

Stein, R. Conrad. *The New Deal: Pulling America Out of the Great Depression*. Berkeley Heights, NJ: Enslow Publishers, Inc., 2006.

BIBLIOGRAPHY

Bannock, Graham, et al. *The Penguin Dictionary of Economics*. 7th ed. New York, NY: Penguin Books, 2003.

Bernanke, Ben S. "Deflation: Making Sure 'It' Doesn't Happen Here." Remarks Before the National Economists Club, Washington, D.C., November 21, 2002. Retrieved August 2009 (http://www.federalreserve.gov/boarddocs/speeches/2002/20021121/default.htm).

Bernanke, Ben S. "Money, Gold, and the Great Depression." Remarks at the H. Parker Willis Lecture in Economic Policy, Washington and Lee University, Lexington, Virginia, March 2, 2004. Retrieved August 2009 (http://www.federalreserve.gov/boarddocs/speeches/2004/200403022/default.htm).

Bonner, Bill, and Addison Wiggin. *Empire of Debt: The Rise of an Epic Financial Crisis*. Hoboken, NJ: John Wiley & Sons, Inc., 2006.

Coy, Peter. "Why the Fed Isn't Igniting Inflation." *Business Week*, June 18, 2009. Retrieved August 2009 (http://www.businessweek.com/magazine/content/09_26/b4137020225264.htm?chan=top+news_top+news+index+-+temp_top+story).

DeLong, J. Bradford. "Slouching Towards Utopia?: The Economic History of the Twentieth Century—XIV. The Great Crash and the Great Slump." Berkeley.edu. Retrieved August 2009 (http://econ161.berkeley.edu/TCEH/Slouch_Crash14.html).

Farrell, Chris. *Deflation: What Happens When Prices Fall.* New York, NY: HarperBusiness, 2004.

Francis, David R. "US Can Avoid Japan's 'Lost Decade' of Deflation." *Christian Science Monitor*, September 28, 2009. Retrieved September 2009 (http://features.csmonitor.com/economyrebuild/2009/09/28/economic-scene-us-can-avoid-japans-lost-decade-of-deflation).

Galbraith, John Kenneth. *The Great Crash 1929.* Boston, MA: Houghton Mifflin Company, 1988.

Gordon, John Steele. *An Empire of Wealth: The Epic History of American Economic Power.* New York, NY: Harper Collins Publishers, 2004.

Irwin, Neil. "Fed to Pump $1.2 Trillion Into Markets." *Washington Post*, March 19, 2009. Retrieved August 2009 (http://www.washingtonpost.com/wp-dyn/content/article/2009/03/18/AR2009031802283.html?hpid=topnews).

Kindleberger, Charles P., and Robert Aliber. *Manias, Panics, and Crashes: A History of Financial Crises.* 5th ed. Hoboken, NJ: John Wiley & Sons, Inc., 2005.

Krugman, Paul. *The Return of Depression Economics.* New York, NY: W. W. Norton and Company, 2009.

Lanigan, Jane, ed. *Economics: Economic History*, vol. 6. Danbury, CT: Grolier Educational, 2000.

Lanigan, Jane, ed. *Economics: Money, Banking, and Finance,* vol. 1. Danbury, CT: Grolier Educational, 2000.

Lynch, David J. "U.S. Can Learn from Japan's Deflated Economy in the 1990s." *USA Today,* January 21, 2008. Retrieved August 2009 (http://www.usatoday.com/money/economy/2008-01-21-japan-parallels_N.htm).

Manmohan, S. Kumar, et al. *Deflation: Determinants, Risks, and Policy Options.* Washington, D.C.: International Monetary Fund, 2003.

Posen, Adam. "Deflationary Lessons: What Japanese Inflation Did and Did Not Do." *International Economy,* Volume 20, issue 1: pp. 20–24. January 2006.

Prechter, Robert R., Jr. *Conquer the Crash: You Can Survive and Prosper in a Deflationary Depression.* Hoboken, NJ: John Wiley & Sons, Inc., 2002.

Rauchway, Eric. *The Great Depression and the New Deal: A Very Short Introduction.* New York, NY: Oxford University Press, 2008.

Riggs, Thomas, ed. *Everyday Finance: Economics, Personal Money Management, and Entrepreneurship.* Farmington Hills, MI: Gale, 2008.

Shilling, A. Gary. *Deflation: How to Survive and Thrive in the Coming Wave of Deflation.* New York, NY: McGraw-Hill, 1999.

Smith, Allen W. *Demystifying Economics: The Book That Makes Economics Accessible to Everyone.* Naples, FL: Ironwood Publications, 2000.

Takeshita, Seijiro. "Japan's Economic Battle with Deflation." BBC News, March 23, 2009. Retrieved August 2009 (http://news.bbc.co.uk/2/hi/business/7955931.stm).

Tanaka, Graham. *Digital Deflation: The Productivity Revolution and How It Will Ignite the Economy.* New York, NY: McGraw-Hill, 2004.

Tucker, Irvin. *Economics for Today.* 3rd ed. Mason, OH: Thomson Learning, 2003.

Wheelan, Charles. *Naked Economics: Undressing the Dismal Science.* New York, NY: W. W. Norton and Company, 2002.

Williams, John C. "The Risk of Deflation." FRBSF Economic Letter, March 27, 2009. Retrieved August 2009 (http://www.frbsf.org/publications/economics/letter/2009/el2009-12.html).

INDEX

About the Author

Corona Brezina has written more than a dozen titles for Rosen Publishing. Several of her previous books have also focused on history and economics, including *The Treaty of Versailles* and *How Stimulus Plans Work*. She lives in Chicago.

Photo Credits

Cover (top) © www.istockphoto.com/Lilli Day; cover (bottom), p. 1 © Alex Wong/Getty Images; pp. 6, 20 © Tim Boyle/Getty Images; pp. 8–9 © David Paul Morris/Getty Images; p. 11 © age fotostock/Superstock; pp. 14–15, 27 © Granger Collection; p. 18 © Michael Nagle/Getty Images; pp. 22–23 © Karen Bleier/AFP/Getty Images; pp. 24–25, 45, 52 © AP Images; p. 31 © Peter Dazeley/Getty Images; pp. 32–33 © David McNew/Getty Images; pp. 36–37 © Emmanuel Dunand/Getty Images; pp. 38–39, 46–47 © Mario Tama/Getty Images; pp. 50–51 © OFF/AFP/Getty Images; p. 55 © Timothy A. Clary/Getty Images; p. 57 © David Young-Wolff; pp. 58–59 © Hulton Archives/Getty Images; pp. 60–61 © Keystone/Getty Images; pp. 64–65 © www.istockphoto.com/Svetlana Tebenkova.

Designer: Sam Zavieh; Photo Researcher: Marty Levick